A Collection of Survivors Stories

Jessica Brown

BookLeaf Publishing

India | USA | UK

Presentation by *BookLeaf Publishing*

Web: www.bookleafpub.com

E-mail: info@bookleafpub.com

ISBN:

First edition 2022

DEDICATION

I dedicate this to every single individual out there with a story of their own.

ACKNOWLEDGEMENT

I'd like to acknowledge all the wonderful survivors who allowed me to use their story to spread awareness. You are strong and did not deserve what happened to you.

PREFACE

Sexual assault, abuse and rape is a major issue in
Australian society, in which almost every female
has a similar story. This also occurs to males and
non-binary individuals. These poems hope to
show how normalises these disgusting
experiences are by making it personal, instead of
a statistic that is haunted by the dark figure of
victims who never report due to fear. It is kept
brief, extremely anonymous and no names will
be listed. Graphic detail was also avoided.
This is no way is intended to trigger anyone, and
thus if this sensitive material is upsetting you,
please don't read this book. My aim is to
empower victims to stand up and tell their story.
Thus, my emails will be open to anyone who
wishes to share their story in which they can't
with the people around them:
jessbrown02@hotmail.com.

Story 1

It was the first few weeks of year seven,
Starting high school to me was like heaven,
But fast enough, you ruined it for me,
By sexualising me to the degree,
Spreading the two boners and horny mood,
That my twelve year old face and looks elude.
Your violation made me feel so fucking,
Uncomfortable and sick it was shocking.

Story 2

I was just thirteen years old with a mate,
Hanging at a park on a fun friend friend date,
And there you were, waiting for some young prey.
You spotted us and decided to say:
"My dick died, can I bury it in you?"
I felt violated because of you.
Who calls that like it's a normal thing to drop?
On unaware young minors left to stew.

Story 3

3

Back in year ten, when you and me fated,
It was about a month we dated,
We did not do sexual relations;
I was a virgin in all dimensions.
But after you ended it randomly,
You painted me as a slut angrily,
Slut-shaming and abusing me always,
Even though you had more sexual liases.

Story 4

4

I let go of a friend because I can,
She didn't take it well and used her man,
To harass and embarrass me for months,
But one events stand out in the long months,
We caught the same bus to school every day,
One morning, he degraded me like prey,
Mocking me as a "dick destroyer" whore,
Even though I hadn't seen one nor more.

Story 5

It was a normal Friday afternoon,
I'm pretty sure it was halfway through June.
I was shopping with my mum and sister,
Texting to kill time at the register.
As random as discerning violet hills,
You sent a picture of hundreds of bills,
In which you wanted to exchange for sex,
As if my body is a priced object.

Story 6

It's a lucky night for me if I don't,
Get asked to send nude pictures that I won't.
Simply saying "no" is not suffice for,
These men that are so desperate for a score.
They beg and beg, attempting to guilt me,
With the unwanted nudes I had to see,
Of their own private area just sent,
As they continue to beg in torment.

Story 7

You were a friend of a friend from running,
Thus, I assumed you would not be cunning.
Nonetheless, you had plans to carry out,
Spreading rumours about me like a spout.
Claiming I desperately asked to fuck you,
When I didn't and definitely didn't want to.
You claimed I was begging for you and that,
Made me feel as worthless as a sick rat.

Story 8

You pretended you had feelings for,
Me for years, as if you felt something more,
With one intention in your cunning mind,
Making sure you had me wrapped in twined.
You took advantage of that and me to,
Get some action and so you could accrue,
A new sex toy you can use when aroused,
Not caring about how I was deceived.

Story 9

I was in no emotional state to,
Make such a sexual decision with you.
I had just been broken up with and I,
Saw my heart break in a blink of an eye.
That one emotional-driven mistake,
Haunted me every second I was awake.
The guilt and knowledge that I was the slut,
Destroyed me inside like a sharp, cold cut.

Story 10

After a long week of college and work,
I let loose at clubs to vanish my irk.
However, the club is full of horny,
And desperate men hunting like an army,
For their new prey they'll offer a drink to,
Thinking that by doing that they can pursue,
Sexual relations, refusing to hear no,
Like a cheap drink is enough to get through.

Story 11

It was a day out with my older sis,
You thought just because you ran the premise,
That by standing on your ground I gave you,
The right to touch and grope me like a beau.
You grabbed my pants area hard and tough,
Saying: "You're a big boy aren't you?" with
gruff,
And you showed no remorse because you did,
It again as if it isn't forbid.

Story 12

As my boyfriend, you thought that meant you gained,
Automatic consent that you obtained,
By simply being a male, as if,
My main role was to satisfy you stiff.
My own pleasure was never your concern,
Because all that time you were acting stern,
In convincing me "blue balls" was real, thus,
I had to protect you from it for "us".

Story 13

Often, mid sexual intercourse I feel,
A light switching off and lose appeal,
To continuing this sexual motion.
Green lighting a dark inner commotion:
Do I keep going for his own pleasure?
Or do I stop for my own displeasure?
And when he notices what's wrong and tries,
To stop for me, I hide my inner cries.

Story 14

14

Seated in the backseat of a friends car,
With you, who our friendship went back way far,
And thus I thought I could trust you deeply,
But the darkness made you act so cheaply,
Grabbing my inner thigh like you'd asked for,
Consent to touch my thigh like that before.
But I was too scared to whisper a word,
When my consent had so far been inferred.

Story 15

15

I was only ten years of age when you,
Utilised cute, stray dogs at the park to,
Lure me and my friend into your home.
You got us alone in your creepy dome,
Taking pictures of us kids in your chair,
And then showing a picture of you bare.
I do not know why, but I kept that print,
And every time I pass you're house, I sprint.

Story 16

As my boyfriend, you thought you had the right,
To my body if you wanted to bite.
My consent and pleasure was misvalued,
As long as you received what you valued.
If I tried to take a stand and say no,
You'd chuck a tantrum like it was such a blow,
Gaslighting me into believing that,
If I didn't, my love for you meant splat.

Story 17

17

As a friend of mine I thought I could trust,
When you asked for naked pictures of just,
My upper breasts and promised not to do,
Anything with the picture I sent you.
However, the second I did send that,
You swooped right in and betrayed me like that,
Screenshotting the photo for all to see,
Not caring about how that'd affect me.

Story 18

I was only young so I had no clue,
That just because I was your loving beau,
It was not okay for you to force me,
Into sex I begged no to in a plea.
You marched me down into the quiet bush,
And made sure my pleas and "no's" were all shush,
Before forcing me to go down on you.
When it circles in my mind I need to spew.

Story 19

19

After years had gone past from your assault,
And years of belief that I was at fault,
I finally realized you had no right,
To force me into sex despite my fight.
I found my voice and spoke out against you,
But everyone refused to believe you,
Would do anything so evil, and thus,
I was a cruel liar causing a fuss.

Story 20

I was twelve when I went on a sea cruise.
I stayed in the kids' part, away from booze.
However, you as a fifteen year old,
Saw my little minor self and you told,
Me I was mature for my age, thus,
You gropped me in a crowd without me fuss,
Because, I was unable to assume,
That this was me being viciously groomed.

Story 21

I was as young as sixteen when you at,
The older age of twenty one, thought that,
You'd put your child fetishes on me;
And I was too young to realise or see,
That this was even wrong for us to do;
That the age gap meant I can't be your beau.
But you took advantage of your power,
Since I was too "mature" to not devour.